C0-APG-832

WITHDRAWN

World Traveler

Travel to

Germany

Christine Layton

Lerner Publications ◆ Minneapolis

For Miranda, Robin, Strudel, and Raisin

Copyright © 2023 by Lerner Publishing Group, Inc.

All rights reserved. International copyright secured. No part of this book may be reproduced, stored in a retrieval system, or transmitted in any form or by any means—electronic, mechanical, photocopying, recording, or otherwise—without the prior written permission of Lerner Publishing Group, Inc., except for the inclusion of brief quotations in an acknowledged review.

Lerner Publications Company
An imprint of Lerner Publishing Group, Inc.
241 First Avenue North
Minneapolis, MN 55401 USA

For reading levels and more information, look up this title at www.lernerbooks.com.

Main body text set in Adrianna Regular.
Typeface provided by Chank.

Map illustration on page 29 by Laura K. Westlund.

Library of Congress Cataloging-in-Publication Data

Names: Layton, Christine Marie, 1985– author.
Title: Travel to Germany / Christine Layton.
Description: Minneapolis : Lerner Publications, [2023] | Series: Searchlight books : world traveler | Includes bibliographical references and index. | Audience: Ages 8–11 | Audience: Grades 4–6 | Summary: "Known for its architecture, landscape, and cuisine, Germany is also a world leader in science and environmentalism. Readers will discover Germany's history and culture through maps, photos, and more!" — Provided by publisher.
Identifiers: LCCN 2022010888 (print) | LCCN 2022010889 (ebook) | ISBN 9781728463964 (pbk.) | ISBN 9781728457895 (lib. bdg.) | ISBN 9781728461946 (eb pdf)
Subjects: LCSH: Germany—Juvenile literature.
Classification: LCC DD17 .L39 2023 (print) | LCC DD17 (ebook) | DDC 943—dc23/eng/20220317

LC record available at https://lccn.loc.gov/2022010888
LC ebook record available at https://lccn.loc.gov/2022010889

Manufactured in the United States of America
1-50817-50156-7/25/2022

Table of Contents

Chapter 1

GEOGRAPHY AND CLIMATE

Germany is a country in central Europe with many different and vibrant landscapes. You can drive along twisty highways and see wide plains with farms or forests where red foxes and wild boars hide among the trees. Hills and tall mountain peaks stand high over medieval castles, villages, and large cities.

Land

Germany borders the Baltic Sea to the northeast and the North Sea to the northwest. It touches Austria, Belgium, the Czech Republic, Denmark, France, Luxembourg, the Netherlands, Poland, and Switzerland.

Germany is one of the largest countries in Europe. It has many landscapes. The mountains in the south are part of the Bavarian Alps. Zugspitze is the highest mountain.

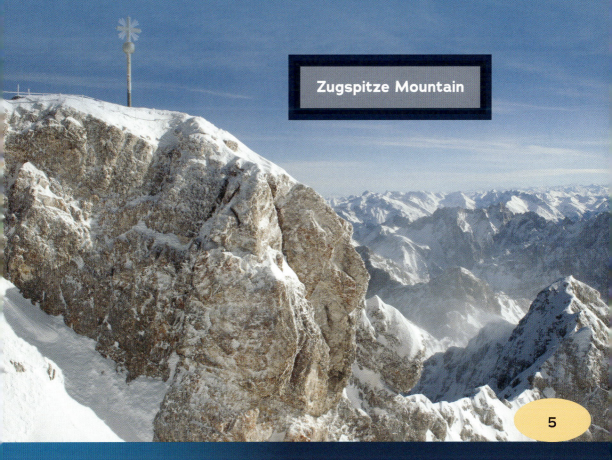

Zugspitze Mountain

Northern Germany has rolling plains. Bogs and mudflats border the plains. The seashore has many islands. Most of Germany's rivers flow north to the sea. But the Danube flows east from the Black Forest to the border of Austria. The Rhine is Germany's longest river. It runs through Lake Constance.

Lake Constance was formed about ten thousand years ago by the Rhine Glacier.

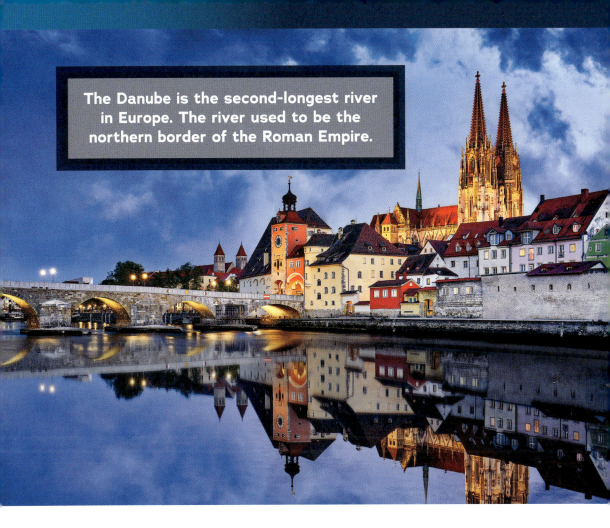

The Danube is the second-longest river in Europe. The river used to be the northern border of the Roman Empire.

The Black Forest is in the southwest. It is a thickly wooded area. Eastern Germany has plains and lots of farmland. Snow melts in the mountains and flows down to join the Danube River.

Germany's land has many natural resources. It has fuels like coal and natural gas. The land holds minerals like iron ore, copper, and nickel. Germany's forests are a source of timber. The soil is good for growing crops and raising livestock.

Must-See Stop:
The Black Forest

Fir, oak, and beech trees grow close together in the Black Forest. The forest covers 2,320 square miles (6,009 sq. km). People in the Black Forest make crafts from lumber. Traditional woodworking is popular. People make watches, musical instruments, and cuckoo clocks. Tourists visit the Black Forest all year long. They ski, snowshoe, and sled in the winter. Visitors swim in springs in the summer.

The Bavarian Alps form the border between Germany and Austria. The mountains provide a great climate for winter sports.

Climate

Germany has a temperate climate. Winters are cool and wet, with lots of rainfall or snowfall across the country. Spring can bring warm or cool weather.

Each area of Germany has its own weather patterns. Wet air moves in from the sea in the north. It makes summers there humid, and fog develops in the winter. The east and center have hotter summers and colder winters than the rest of the country. The mountains in the south get lots of snow and rain.

Germany's weather is changing as climate change causes new weather patterns such as severe rainstorms and floods. Such weather events are happening in Germany more often than in the past.

Chapter 2

HISTORY AND GOVERNMENT

Archaeologists have found artifacts in bogs that show people have lived in Germany since the Bronze Age around 1700 BCE. The soft, wet land in bogs can keep wood, leather, and even some skeletons from rotting for years. This helps archaeologists learn more about how ancient people lived in Germany.

Early Germany

Early Germanic tribes traded with the Romans, exchanging amber and leather for Roman pottery, glass, and metal. The Frankish Empire brought together the Germanic tribes around the year 500. Royal families in the Middle Ages ruled the area for hundreds of years. They built castles across the country. This area became known as the Holy Roman Empire in 1254.

MEERSBURG CASTLE

▼

At that time, France, Prussia, Austria, and Russia fought over the hundreds of small states and cities that made up Germany. In 1806, the French leader Napoleon took over a large area of Europe, including many German states and cities. Napoleon was later defeated, but the war brought German people together. The people in this area started to call themselves Germans.

The German Empire formed on January 18, 1871, led by an emperor, or kaiser. As the empire grew, it joined other European countries in colonizing regions of Africa, Asia, and the Pacific Ocean.

In 1904, the German Empire suppressed a revolt in present-day Namibia and killed many of the Herero and Nama people. The military forced the survivors into slavery.

Armies in World War I dug trenches along the front lines. They would charge across the dangerous and unoccupied area between the trenches.

Germany Divided

In World War I (1914–1918), the German Empire, Austria-Hungary, and Turkey fought against Britain, France, and the Russian Empire. The German Empire lost the war. They lost a lot of land and all of their colonies.

The German people faced many challenges because of World War I and the Great Depression. People lost jobs. Businesses closed. In 1933, Adolf Hitler and the Nazi Party came to power. Hitler promised to fix all of Germany's problems.

Hitler led Germany into World War II (1939–1945). Germany, Italy, and Japan fought against Britain, the Soviet Union (fifteen republics that included Russia), and the United States. Millions of people died. The Nazis killed about six million Jewish people and hundreds of thousands of others, such as the Roma and Sinti people. Jews were blamed for all of Germany's problems. In the end, Germany lost the war.

In 1941, the German government forced Germans of Jewish descent to wear yellow badges in the shape of the Star of David.

East and West Germany opened their shared border on November 9, 1989. The wall was demolished by boarder guards and local Germans.

Germany Reunited

Other countries divided Germany to limit the country's power. The country was split into East Germany and West Germany. East Germany built the Berlin Wall between them. West Germany was a democracy supported by the US. East Germany was a Communist state supported by the Soviet Union.

In 1989, East Germany's Communist government ended. People tore down the Berlin Wall, and thousands of Germans crossed the border. East and West Germany officially came together again in 1990.

Let's Celebrate:
German Unity Day

German Unity Day is a national holiday. Germans celebrate it on October 3 each year. On that day, East and West Germany came together again. People spend Unity Day with their friends and family. Many have picnics in national parks to celebrate. German Unity Day has a festival called Bürgerfest. Actors, comedians, and musicians perform. People sell food, drinks, and sweets. Fireworks light up the sky.

Reichstag, Berlin

Government

The sixteen states that make up Germany are called the Federal Republic of Germany. Germany has a constitution. This is a list of rules and rights for the people and government.

The government is a federal parliamentary republic. A parliament makes laws and elects the leader of the German government, the chancellor. The chancellor is the commander in chief of the German military during wartime. The chief of state is the president, who is elected by a special assembly every five years. The president helps keep the government running and travels the world to represent Germany. German people vote for the members of parliament.

Chapter 3

CULTURE AND PEOPLE

Most Germans have German ancestors. Some German people have Syrian, Turkish, or Romanian ancestors. Many people also immigrate to Germany. They come from places like Turkey, the Middle East, and North Africa.

Almost everyone in Germany speaks German. Some people speak Danish, Frisian, Sorbian, Romani, and Turkish. There are many local German dialects too. Many people speak multiple languages!

Religion

Christianity is the most popular religion in Germany. About half of Christians are Protestant. The other half are Roman Catholic. Immigrants bring other religions to Germany. About 5 percent of Germans are Muslim. Germany's Jewish population is growing too. About one hundred thousand Jewish people live in Germany. Not everyone in Germany is religious. About one out of every three Germans is not religious.

The building of the Cologne Cathedral was started in 1248 CE. It wasn't fully complete until 1880 CE.

Let's Celebrate:
Christmas Season

Winter brings many celebrations. Germans start to celebrate at Advent around December 1. They decorate with wreaths. People bake gingerbread houses, cookies, and cakes. Germans celebrate Saint Nicholas Day on December 6. Children clean their rooms and toys. They polish their shoes and set them out by the door. Children find

candy, gold coins, and small treats in their shoes in the morning. Germans celebrate Christmas on December 24. They usually have a family dinner, sing carols, and open gifts.

German bakeries are full of many kinds of bread, from Roggenmischbrot (rye bread) to Weißbrot (white bread) to the many varieties of Brötchen (bread rolls).

Food

Traditional German food has many breads and sausages. Wurst is a German sausage. People eat wurst all over Germany. There are over fifteen hundred kinds of wurst. People enjoy wurst with sauerkraut. Sauerkraut is pickled cabbage.

German baking includes breads, pretzels, and pastries. Brötchen is a popular bread. Brötchen are small rolls. Bakers sprinkle them with seeds or nuts. Many people eat

Spargel (white asparagus) is picked in the spring during Spargelzeit. Many cities have festivals to celebrate the season.

them for breakfast. Brötchen are also buns for bratwurst. Bratwurst is like a hot dog with different spices.

German meals also have seasonal vegetables. White asparagus, or Spargel in German, is very popular. It even has its own season, Spargelzeit.

Music

German music is popular around the world. Many Germans wrote famous classical music. Johann Sebastian Bach and Ludwig van Beethoven are famous German composers. Orchestras and operas are still popular in Germany.

Let's Celebrate:
Oktoberfest

Oktoberfest is one of the world's largest festivals. More than five million people go each year. It's from late September through the first Sunday in October. People celebrate Oktoberfest every year in Bavaria, Germany. Oktoberfest begins with a parade. The festival features traditional German clothing, music, and food. Visitors eat chicken, roast pork, sausages, and large pretzels called Brezeln.

Volksmusik means "music of the people." Guitars and harmonicas may accompany these folk songs. Oompah music gets its name from the thumping sounds of the tuba. This music also uses accordions. Volksmusik and oompah music are very popular in Germany.

Marlene Dietrich was a German actor and singer who used her fame to help Jews escape from Germany in the 1930s.

Chapter 4

DAILY LIFE

Germany is the second most populated country in Europe after Russia. Many people live in large cities. In cities, most people live in apartments or condos. Houses are expensive.

Germany is a mix of old and new. In the mountains, people still celebrate the return of cattle in the spring. They have a festival and parade. People practice local arts like carving wood and making violins. Some women wear traditional clothes called a Tracht on festival days.

Economy

Germany has the fifth-largest economy in the world. Germans make machinery and vehicles. They also make chemicals and household goods. Germans export these goods to the rest of the world. Germany is one of the top exporters in the world along with China and the United States.

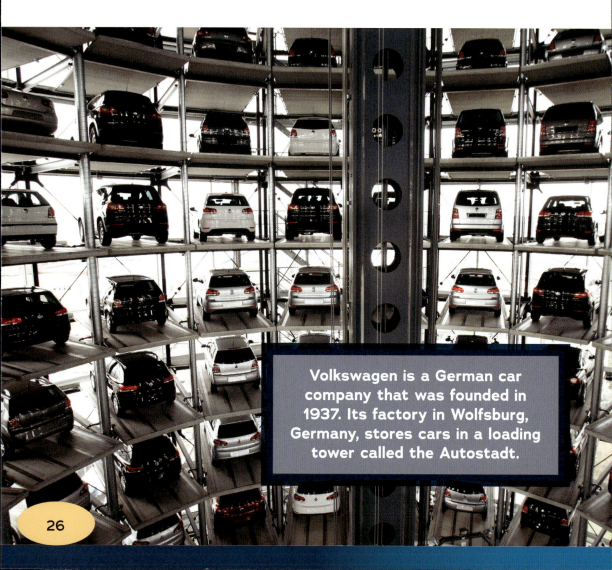

Volkswagen is a German car company that was founded in 1937. Its factory in Wolfsburg, Germany, stores cars in a loading tower called the Autostadt.

Must-See Stop:
Neuschwanstein Castle

Neuschwanstein Castle sits on a cliff in the Bavarian Alps. Construction of the castle for Ludwig II started in 1868. The Bavarian king died before the builders finished. The unfinished castle became a tourist spot. Neuschwanstein Castle is different from many German castles. The castle looks medieval. But it has hot running water, heated air, and toilets. An elevator travels three stories from the kitchen to the dining room.

Germany generates a lot of wind power with over twenty-eight thousand wind turbines. Many wind turbines are offshore in the North Sea.

Plans for the Future

The German government has many plans for Germany's future. One goal is to use green energy to slow down climate change. For example, German automobile factories will make electric cars. Germany will use more solar panels and wind energy. The government plans to stop using coal for energy.

Germany will continue to develop and grow in the future. But Germans will also keep the traditions of the past alive.

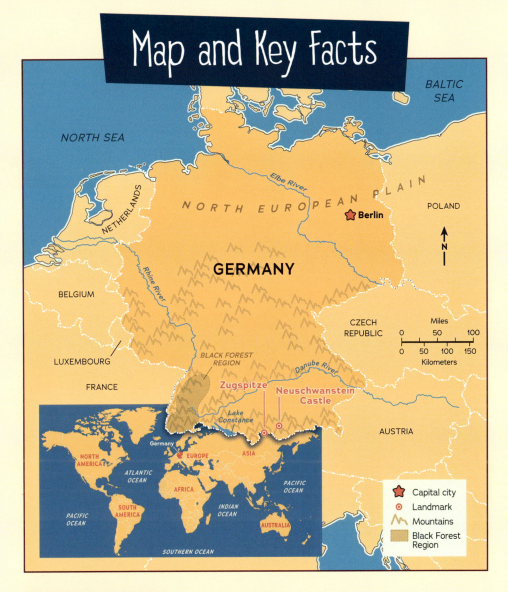

BALTIC SEA

NORTH SEA

NETHERLANDS

Elbe River

NORTH EUROPEAN PLAIN

★ Berlin

POLAND

N

GERMANY

BELGIUM

Rhine River

CZECH REPUBLIC

Miles
0   50   100
0   50 100 150
Kilometers

LUXEMBOURG

BLACK FOREST REGION

Danube River

Zugspitze

Neuschwanstein Castle

FRANCE

Lake Constance

AUSTRIA

Germany
NORTH AMERICA
EUROPE
ASIA
ATLANTIC OCEAN
AFRICA
PACIFIC OCEAN
PACIFIC OCEAN
SOUTH AMERICA
INDIAN OCEAN
AUSTRALIA
SOUTHERN OCEAN

★ Capital city
⊙ Landmark
⋀⋀ Mountains
▧ Black Forest Region

Flag of Germany

- **Continent: Europe**
- **Capital city: Berlin**
- **Population: 83,155,031**
- **Languages: German and many regional languages**

Glossary

ancestor: a member of a family who lived long ago

BCE: an abbreviation of before the common era; used to show dates in history

bog: an area of soft, wet land

colony: a territory that is controlled by another country

Communist state: a government where the land and resources belong to the government

democracy: a government where the people choose their leaders in an election

dialect: a form of a language that is spoken in a certain region or by a certain group

export: to send products to another country to sell them there

immigrate: to go to another country to live permanently

republic: a government where the people elect representatives who manage the government

temperate: when the temperature is rarely very high or very low

Learn More

Britannica Kids: Germany
    https://kids.britannica.com/kids/article/Germany/345694

Dean, Jessica. *Germany*. Minneapolis: Pogo, 2019.

Kallen, Stuart A. *World War II Spies and Secret Agents*. Minneapolis: Lerner Publications, 2018.

Kids World Travel Guide: Germany
    https://www.kids-world-travel-guide.com/germany-facts.html

National Geographic Kids: Germany
    https://kids.nationalgeographic.com/geography/countries/article /germany

Venezia, Mike. *Ludwig van Beethoven*. New York: Children's Press, 2017.

Index

Photo Acknowledgments

Image credits: olga.syrykhShutterstock, p. 5; Nick Biemans/Shutterstock, p. 6; Harald Nachtmann/Getty Images, p. 7; Matyas Rehak/Shutterstock, p. 8; Westend61/Getty Images, p. 9; fotolinchen/Getty Images, p. 11; © Government of the Republic of Namibia, p. 12; Historica Graphica Collection/Heritage Images/Getty Images, p. 13; Sueddeutsche Zeitung Photo/ Alamy Stock Photo, p. 14; Justin LeightonAlamy Stock Photo, p. 15; Jan Woitas/picture alliance/ Getty Images, p. 16; querbeet/Getty Images, p. 17; Bernhard Klar/EyeEm/Getty Images, p. 19; michelsass/Getty Images, p. 20; Alan Gleichman/Shutterstock, p. 21; juefraphoto/Getty Images, p. 22; moreimages/Shutterstock, p. 23; Bettmann/Getty Images, p. 24; AP Photo/Joerg Sarbach,File, p. 26; Frank Fischbach/Shutterstock, p. 27; CharlieChesvick/Getty Images, p. 28; Laura K. Westlund, p. 29.

Cover image: joe daniel price/Getty Images.

CONTRA COSTA COUNTY LIBRARY

31901069917732